also by OLI HAZZARD
from Carcanet

Between Two Windows (2012)

BLOTTER

OLI HAZZARD

CARCANET

First published in Great Britain in 2018 by
Carcanet Press Ltd
Alliance House, 30 Cross Street
Manchester M2 7AQ

A CIP catalogue record for this book is available from the British Library, ISBN 9781784105303

Design: Luke Allan. Typeset by Richard Skelton.
Printed & bound in England by SRP Ltd.

The publisher acknowledges financial assistance from Arts Council England.

CONTENTS

GRAIG SYFYRDDIN

or EDMUND’S TUMP

Dawn of Day on minor road to east – easy parking in unused gate entrance. Very much stands on its own with extensive views all round. Started at the entrance to Dawn of Day at Cross Ash. Nice gentle climb up the edge of fields to trig point. Would be fine views on a clear day but somewhat hazy today. From start of drive to dawn of day which i thought was going to be a sculpture. Walked up drive to Dawn of the Day, realised mistake and restarted on footpath on south side of their fence. Sign hidden in hedge IIRC. Operated SOTA from near the weather station. From east on FP by entrance to 'DOW' then left and followed fence to top and trig point. great views in all directions. From minor road to East, ROW past The Dawn of Day. Walk up field, through wood and across pasture. Fabulous views with plenty of bluebells

about midday
        I turn on
myself. Heat
        clingfilms
a band
        of air
on the hill.
        What I saw
was maybe
        nothing
else but
        reversed
the unfinished
        state
in which spring
        leaves
the air
        between
branches
        too

Parked on wide verge of minor road to W. (SO39567 20951) – Crossed road, climbed stile and took footpath up to stile into woods – Up through woods & across sheep pasture to trig point. (PM) Parked at 395210. An eventual ascent east into the woods before meeting atrack through the forest. I turned left for a short distance before heading up through the coniferous trees to the open top. With GB. 6/7 Park to west at bend in road and follow track up steep slopes to forest.

whiten
I decline, polite
to acknowledge

like a bell that doesn't strike

imperfect
elaborate
and forget

In forest head to right off track to top cross fence to trig pillar After an interesting stay in the Hope and Anchor at Ross on Wye, (great breakfast but the accommodation block has sloping floors and the external walls have several cracks) we were hoping for the weather to improve. Rain had stopped but still very foggy so I cant say much about this one as we couldn't see further than 20m

Thursday
I tried to delete
a speck of soup
on the screen

many-bonneted foxglove
like a cloud of future garments
down the steepest
invisible staircase

beneath flattened early evening
petri-dishy sky says
this page pre changes
has 'finger-like' for the ease
with which a flower of
digitalis purpurea
can be fitted over a human
fingertip

My thoughts about boats

are boats

Started up path from west. From Grosmont village. Followed paths through fields and a wood to the east of the summit. Took a sneaky shortcut through a field with no ROW to pick up the path up the ridge to the summit. Back via the track through the forest. As per David Gradwell route – straightforward through pasture and woodland higher up. From road junction, up and down via three castle way. Up ProW to side of Dawn of Day for SOTA with Geoff Fielding. Up from lay-by in Cross Ash. Nice views towards Abergavenny. Bit hazy, but lovely views of Sugar Loaf, Blorenge and Skirrid. Need to find a route through the conifers to get to the summit, but possible. Followed the 3 castles walk over the hill Climbed from the eastern side. Straightforward. up track past house to domed top – mind the dogs! With Shaun Whittaker.

starts snow
ing—sort
of emptily—
minor explosion
at the vowel
factory—
never liked
these things

so much
            as now
they're in
            my mouth—rain
in the valleys—snow
            on the peak

More drops from nose.
Nausea plateaus.
And breathing out
the grain of
the wood of
the air

radiant with imaginary jewels
like a person listening closely

January falls on the roof that isn't there

In 1802 March 3rd was a Wednesday.
Like ribbons of toothpaste from a tube.
Seems like I'm heading south.

o

never liked such
ow they're in my mouth

Parked at 249 junction and took path through field and into wood to track. Walked S then straight up through wood to open summit field. Dry, good views. Lots of bluebells in wood. Finished 16:50 Parked on rough verge at SO 39572 20924. Public footpath through fields to stile at edge of wood. Steep section to track in wood. Turned right then left on small path to open fields. Turned left to stile then diagonally across sheep pasture to trig. From SW in the early morning dew. Took a direct route up from the east having parked opposite the entrance to Dawn of Day Cottage.

. . . in Nash's photo of the Abbey
        it's seventeen ninety eight,
my forehead's imprint on the window
        slowly becoming visible. In

its 1939, and the leaves
        in the foreground obscure where
the Abbey meets the earth, as though it
        had floated free of its age

or descended momentarily
        to give instruction to what
shall I call you. I don't know if con
        cealing the join between earth and

building points to an old desire
        to float free of history
or in floating free gestures better
        toward what is excluded from the

image, but the word wavers between
        a noun and a verb. The night
you were born I imagined I saw
        the time after you before

you arrived in the poem I pour
        my ill-fitting poem into,
breaking the banks of the river the
        train passes a splayed mirror beneath

toward the sky, a field . . .

Boring climb but nice views from the top and very moody with black clouds building up to the N. At gateway saying 'Dawn of Day Cottage'. Good track up hill into open field with trig at top. Space to park on minor road at bottom of ROW near 249 spot height. Approached from SW via two fields then through woods and into top field to bag top and trig point. Good views today in moody weather. Great views. A good example of how nice a Marilyn can be.

A log cabin

in the shopping centre
impenitent

as the weather
vanishing behind the words for it

pip pip

the Bay of Fundy

plain as pain
in its element

Parked at 249. Accessed from the SW, good views on a dry sunny morning. Pleasant stroll – lots of mist and saw nothing. Absolutely fantastic panoramic views all the way around. I wish i lived in that bungalow near the top

face down
to the ground
panoramic views all the way around

but I was talking about trains
how they facilitate collaboration, that it
is impossible to tell which poet wrote which line

which is a line, of course, I can tell, or I think
outside the window it's 1965
and that to be stationary and in motion at once
I say, in my first lecture, which is my interview
presentation regurgitated
is what reading is like, how time is layered
into the paint. In the lecture
the poet died, and I didn't know him well enough
but I can, just from the little inflections
catch myself completing the sentence
incorrectly: but that's not where I was
going in the dark, in the poem
it's possible to see one poet teaching the other
to look out of the window, to say
did you really understand what I meant by that

never lied

the thin

snow its in my

moth

Started at 7.10 am from just south of the 249m spot height on the minor road. Up via the footpath managing to slip of stile and gash my leg good start. Trig found easily despite low level cloud. Having seen Robin nr Oxford after his climbing accident with broken legs (now mended) drove to Ross on Wye – slept in car, up at 6.30 am – lovely sunrise Up through fields and wood to summit. Drove back t Sheffield. Full of cold

There I am
my little dick
tickling a theramin
watching the little sails (?)

on the glossy horizon

('the horizon of
glossolalia')

come in.

Is what already
it day

hill
even weather skim-reads

550' up over sheep pastures and into wood. Extensive felling made for a vigorous scramble over fallen boughs and debris to grassy dome. Date is first visit. Notes from later...messy route but pleasant hill (albeit in mist & near-dark). FP from 396209, find way thru conifers to summit pasture From SW via woods. Turnips in field @ top. Small bagging trip with brother, we made it a leisure drive for Mom as well. Parked at space on minor road at bottom of ROW near pt. 249m, up ROW from there and to trig point in pasture, just of ROWs. Cloudy, fair views. Did Garway Hill, just 6 km away, after lunch. Superb views all round – Malverns, Bredon Hill, Black Mountain, Abergavenny 3 Peaks, Cleeve Hill & Mendips all visible from trig point in middle of field (S6428) Missed footpath sign and ended up outside bungalow where we were confronted by owner. We explained our error and we were redirected back to the road and the path which runs parallel with the driveway to the aforementioned bungalow. Otherwise, no problem other than summit in cabbages. Up here in the snow

New York, 11 June 2016

MARCH AND MAY

true, this

morning washes

its face in

the light's

a distant

sensation

beneath

the keys

for desire

to escape

close life

in favour

of whatever

single ringing

note

presents

when one

word sees

itself in another

August ignites

light floats

in the room

I rent

wait

nocturnal note

up at 6

day softening

in the bowl

some pages

are omitted from

the summer

some things

I admit are over

tomorrow

a refrain I hum

over a fact

subsiding

there's no

will my eye

stoops to graze

this mirage

my tongue

runs over

the dunes

of the roof

of my mouth

in the

out of sight

I refrain from

thinking

since I live

only by you

thinking of me

changing

and personal

and awake

what I'm looking

at for

to throw myself

to my knees

colour as it dries

a stressful dream

I would have

loved to share

as I recall both

you and I

were there

in my lunch hour

on castle beach

I liked

an industrial

ship, genus

awkward

the horizon

like the silent p

in receipt

of indifference

is historical

before myself

and be shared

no, to get

but to go

so long without

understanding

each other

when we do

it unnerves

the vowels

looping

around the

knuckles

until the

circulation

pauses

anxious over

the menu, true

late and pale

5 years

of addresses

up to 83 percent

of dreams

contain some colour

reaching for

that keeps me

so nearly afloat

on a blurting

moment, no

still more

remotely

he's talking

now

without words

and I can't think

of anything

I'd rather say

so just sit

here and hear

him singing

many of her notes

are sounds

like when you ask

what I'm doing

and I hesitate

and say 'working'

an activity

whose name I am

that cannot be

written

the alphabet

having no

letters that can

syllable

the sounds

Clare writes

of the

nightingale

in the orchard

in Northborough

there's which I was thinking

a depression of last night

in my address as you came

I had to wait to stop myself

to write from working

my phone's dead from home

a prolonged pause

before I remember

the day, like

I can't believe

I couldn't believe

it's finished

try in an hour

try tonight

remind me

tomorrow

is there

running its

stirring it up

and just

staring

at a love poem

life sways

away from

finger around

the rim of

a wine glass

creepily

small acts

of disgrace

that save

the date

true, I don’t believe

in it

because I am it

rather than

universal desire

in its unselfconscious

state

light in the cloud

snow in a

stirrup

a falling leaf

on the palely

queueing air

wait, it hurts

happiness exists

that this is

possible

that it will stop

being possible

this wanting

to mean

I'm happy

at the vastly

morning

by just

turning

seriously

fuck who I am

is how

I'd ask you

to fuck me

unseasonably

stilted in

period speech

off enough
        to march
some pages
        are omitted
while it's
        may, true
the word
        shapen
happens
        sharpens
how I see
        the snow
how I know
        it is
what it is
        only listening
to it glistening
        in the air

I put a
        spell on
because I'm
        in stony fetters
fixed and clicking
        getting myself

of the word
        no, wait
calling in sick
        for each other
in each other's
        fake sick voices

in sympathy

I lack

except here

the weakness

protecting

the time

debris prised

from debris

still, achey

little aperture

this huge hill

somersaults

good life

choices

the murmuring

of numerable

bees

vanishing

into the fiction

of a person

I am tired

of not becoming

unbecoming

to float like that

through

    it's starting to rain

like someone

    trying not to

panic

    it's raining

my form

    and the day

screamed

    along its seams

slept through it

    letting light in

still coming

    with a terrible

plainness

    momentarily

into view

    then fading

with an equally

    terrible alacrity

the clarity

    of an anagram

the clouds

    perform

like the form

    I was made

me say

    I was made

to say

    this by

to slowly

    patrol the floor

like a hand

    meticulously

smoothing

    a crease

true, I've

    had it too

one tiny love

    revolving

in the green

    of a never

more particular

    morning

developing

    quite abruptly

in real time

    about

the splash

    of an abbey

disappearing

    into the green

pageantry

    of the year

off the coast

there was

what

true, my love

sailed

calmly on

WITHIN HABIT

the density of archaeological sites in the British landscape is so great that a line drawn through virtually anywhere will 'clip' a number of sites

Archaeological Theory: An Introduction

You there – I – here
With just the Door ajar
That Oceans are –

Emily Dickinson

We read too much | into the ground | beneath | the ground beneath our feet. Since everything that happened | happened there | it bombed. Who knows what | Power failed along the lines. But like Christopher Newman (a character | in Henry James's *The American*) I prefer the copies | of masterpieces | over the originals. As Paul Nash implied | perhaps to distinguish the trees | from the wood, its bark is worse than | as Lee Harwood might say | all you do, my | is appropriate. You mine | my mine | with yours. Steel yourself | for an act of originality

bite

that feeds it. The divisions | undivided | all the sweeter. I was intimated across the threshold | of a margin | of a centre | moved by the accents of a margin | a kind of latent relief. | Something both doubtable and redoubtable | a reliquary of limits. You could snooze by the light | of such names | and this is no | library, chief. Beware po-faced Ƿōden for he knows | not what you do: the kind of case prefaced by head or | nut of the Brazilian | variety. A little distance quakes under its cost. Who | *will fly me now?* Asks | poor Monmouth, sweltering | in the rain | of his name.

At any one time there are as many different | types of music as there are rooms | to pay tribute to | sealing them from one another. Poorly fitted doors mean | to feign intimacy through | that from a certain position it is possible | to hear Bartok resisting | the traffic slowing speech muffled | a mouthful | of ketchup and | jam. In the square they fail | openly, too convincingly | to achieve a system perfected in its journey across | the assent of many | senses. Touching in its | simplicity the hearts and | lawns of council offices the opening

joins

these two people | to the moment. You may kiss | the winter with your new lips | may remain | the silence of | resolution to ignore your example. Streets | contradict the speech of | never again to tolerate the | astronomical entry price | for high | violence and its music across the | water. High over the school or office | makeshift barricades are erected within | nothing. A logic beyond capacity to prove need through | exhaustion of any defence | of flowers, their continual definition | of a gesture outside the block of | language just down the road from where we | live.

In the space of a few lines | you may find yourself | in the space of a few lines | roomy enough to dwell in | some cloudy morning—the little adjustments | falling makes | in the receptacle | from which the desire to receive | somatic perfume | of the pressure drops halfway through | the sentence | make themselves felt as distinctions from a state | of deep sleep | landscaping. Working as agents induces an improper feeling of flatness | sex flowers strike | so light it hardly registers as defeat | the tears or weak areas. To determine the appropriate pressure | for

movement

to be deterred | partition calls back the candelabra-form espalier called a palmette verrier | from which falls | at close intervals a downpour of | stops. High over | an area of rainforest | makeshift barricades are erected | to distinguish the trees | from the wood to form a thick, impenetrable | paywall | against environs. At the touch of your | music | ash dissolves harmlessly | as though from a great height | to reveal the shape of | my own hand holding | my own hand holding | my own hand back from | its element. Meliboeus, please, we all make mistakes | the price of | watching their flight.

Twin weather | backs out the corridor | hands aloft | to signal retrace stops | to modulate her walk to | a dancing step. The lapse between that | which is inscribed | torques on its broadside | tmesis or, how the barrier enhances | the emphasis towards | experience. Bound by the usable | parts of animals | Henry James | does not divide into hands nor the face into faces | developing into cries | at birth indicating the airway is clear of mucus. I thought that | by the lashing of young growth to straight sticks and binding the joints | I could say | while I care | I don't

repeat the pattern

think | I believe. I thought that | cloud. There's something difficult in my simple solution binding problem. Valley fold | the top left corner over to the right as shown. Crease well. Unfold the paper, then repeat the last fold on the other side of the | palmette verrier. Do a mountain fold horizontally though the intersection | of the crease marks | to make a diagonal lattice | alongside the things | it shows to be dependent upon | a backing track | across the sound the breeze makes | To keep | the screen | awake, Thiersch preferred the term 'inosculation', derived from the Latin *inosculare*, to kiss.

As shock is | buffering | the moving object | a fold remembers as kind of cooled by water | from the competing source | No news is. I have driven | my experience | to distraction | for the weekend in the hope that | like mouths meeting | it may not come to notice my absence. To prevent | Monmouth from coming | to before the anaesthetic has worn off | keep talking to the dream like a child telling itself | it's not real. It's not | how long it is but what you do with it that counts | itself a forward motion of | regress related to the duration | of the film of the | With your

face

book open in another tab, like we're in different rooms in the same house | neither of us owns | nobody enters without warning. Face to hand | to face. It's not | waking up in the middle of the operation I'm afraid | the surgeon is asleep. There is loud music somewhere behind the wall | in the next flat | young fruit trees are pruned to purpose. Whichever of us two you first behold | assumes the shape of the object's absence | to keep the screen awake click | when the cloaked wearer moves | my mouth starts watering | an unfolded map of | an area of rainforest the size of | thy carcase.

We can't expect to watch it live | in its 'natural habitat' | and ask a perfect stream | gathered at the banks of | to experience | a coming together | determined by the season | in a platonic bed shared by tragedy. As Paul Nash implied | the materials for aphorism should be supplied | without instruction | to raise water cannon. The divisions are implied | but exceed the absent border | where prices fall imperceptibly | about the head, a regimen of severe seasonal relativism. Is it evaporating or snowing | an arrangement structured by the objects partially

obscured

by the weather? I have taken this | image without asking what it's for specific purposes | protozoa in the water | system develops a treatment derived from cells of | Henry James, inosculated | to the yielding plainness started out as. There was a reason for contiguity to receive the call to | speak up, for itself, for | as a whole made of pieces bringing precise objects | out of focus | into play. All kinds of wrong gestures | Meliboeus prescribes the | weight, elevated upon the scaffold high over the city | become, like mouths meeting | in the space of a few lines | a laughter track | to tell | flowers by.

Working as agents within their cultural constraints, but cognizant of those constraints, they saw | themselves as though from a great height | projected onto a screen above | a compulsion to see | in their own appearance | patterns such as stained glass | a remix of a remix of | a see-saw. The interference of frequencies by combining different tracks | describes the wave in little grains, putting more or less space between | a particular place where it always rains: or something like | a piercing shaft of light | changing the colour of my eyes | during gestation | my opinions of the

hanging styles

have changed so much since the time of its composition | it is necessary to kneel in order to see as intended. I extend my hand to shake your | rubber hand | extends the | region which falls under the jurisdiction of your | body, yes | it is necessary to kneel in order to cry loudly and repeatedly, clearing fluid and opening air to form a thick, impenetrable negative | against its environs. At the touch of your rubber on my | eyes, I experience the sensation of floating above my own hand | holding a shell | in which the sound of the sea may be heard | now only intermittently.

Derived from the sound of the | valve, like a | piercing shaft of light blinks describe the choice | now only intermittently | a regimen of severe | spatial blurring. Here lies | the field across which patterns such as people appeared | to feign intimacy in appearance, a particular place where | my mouth starts watering | house prices | we appear happy to eat | adjacency within. At which point Christopher | holds his manifold | breath up to the glass fibre mold | breaks on impact with | a wax boy | a piercing shaft of little adjustments. Floated in | a cage of days | *as a wave moves*

onward

but the water of which it is composed does not | The unity of birds' nests is only phenomenal. The water recalls | how to recall | the patient described earlier | in the language | of the manual | who would panic and gasp for breath whenever | it rained for years. Hu mans, presumably, will retain control of | the glass fibre mold | 'as a flower springs in a fenced garden'. For years a delay | implied across the water | in the next room | is moving a hand | over the meadow to create the sign | of a polylactic | joke, responded to promptly like mouths meeting | with a cloth placed over the forehead and eyes.

Throughout the | jackpot | is worn | a mingled stuff | that creates | the illusion of | an arrow passing through the head. The level features coloured bricks | clouds flickering | pipes from which flower flowers that eat | a ventoused skull that protrudes | inwards away from the Greek. It was noted | The capacity was exceeded in the meadow | Somebody's name | swayed from the pale in vested limits | antiquity's breeze pilfered | from a clusterfuck of a rig. *What have you got there?* | is where my bikini | was made episcopal | went bald in a hot wind | yard. The worst

night

of | laurel patch | is taken out | to understand the entire scene | as though from a great height | it falls from appropriation. Monmouth legs are sleeping | with the fishes | sleeping in his legs. Today I ply the injured drum | to montage the prose of | natural wear faltering slowly. How do you sleep | yourself in the eye | at night to the sound of dolphins | mourning? The absent spire | in the water forms a pattern | to escape through | to divert from | towards the water where the lines used to be. Are we there | Meliboeus somewhere in the background of the | yet?

We extend our hands | to form enclosures | within Monmouth as though | being unable to express it | a kind of latent relief. Whichever of us you first behold | confused by kindness | extend your hand | to verify the hole through which | the medium is falling apart from itself. Here lies | fall out in a glass fibre mold | roomy enough to dwell in | solution. I don't know why there aren't more words for | sorry, its different gradations | depressed by overuse. If say it | against something else | like mouths meeting | slowly gradual, so as that no progress is | hoped for, only

the hope

to keep the screen awake | it will be subsequently absorbed into the body | in a gentle gesture | of completion. If you look | peristaltic the pressure drops halfway through | the shooting | make themselves felt as protrusions | from a state | to escape into | starts moving. High over the | wild lawn | of the land parts, allows | its children to descend into private | constraint placed about the head. To compensate for the extrusion of the scaffold | the content floats in the form of a menu | to laugh | behind the depictions of | depictions of | leaves on the skin.

We paused long enough to | be heard. After all there is a shadowy something—akin to what the painter's call one's air—hovering about the | spring: isn't there a pronoun for this indoor sunset | in a different signature | across the water | as clay pottery has also been found bearing rope-shaped protrusions? The goal of cloaking—in fact its very definition—is, however, to make an object less detectable | too convincingly, so that the concealment is coyly declared. But since there was no 'site' | Thiersch preferred to experience it everywhere. 'Artefacts without context are

useless

since the motion couldn't be figured | the presentation was allegiance | combining 1% of the | borborygmic spectrum to produce a complexion | more original than the original. The officers sat in a room together to compose without | within. I watch that necessary aperture | photoshopped into | the language of the family of the pigment | to be heard. It is in fact a better-than-exact replica because the missing piece—the bit that was knocked out when they opened the tomb—we have recreated. So in fact we have made it slightly more original than the original.

Throughout the history of articulation agreements | violence takes the form by | the native rhythm of | the neck of the woods | creamy scout patrols return from unscathed but | unscathed. Similarly, the task of reconquering | the abandoned urban land has been linked by a series of frantic hand gestures | to the decline of | the green/blue palace | nothing changed. The movement was determined by | auto-complete following the presence of | stolen water into | the postcode from which it had only ever partially withdrawn. Look, no faces. It could have been

anything

in the shape of a heart | breaking choice. It could have been | the epithalamion absorption has proved fit | to rule. It's not stealing if it's taken | to be lost. How could that crude | flash off the internal precipice | not be bent | as some kind of casual association absorbs complicity into | a program? Stop me if you've | rebuffed the syntax's selvage. A delicate series of remarks stiffens | passion's reprieve as a late | matrix to swing | lucky crops from. Like always before the refrain | as light draining from a dream | flops access, a flower mouth guard against | not not not not not not | what you mean.

I want to be near you | via nearness generally | an app 'chance' rather than 'skill' | determining the tax obligations of the feathers as | one falls into the pixel | on the white water | interlude. A grid is applied to the | field which dissolves into | the screen harmlessly beneath a summer storm. Shit. The silence that precedes an aperture opening | Left hands of right handed engineers flensed | skittish with false lines. These tears or weak areas | in crying fire | are lined with a very transparent low weight enamel found in the company (from the Latin

com-, 'with,'

and *panis*, 'bread') of other expressions | of space before choice under an ornamental plain. Since the location of paradise seems to be roughly that of Japan, a grid is applied | to the image from which the object had been extracted | and begins to spurt. As Emerson says, lyrical, not epical or even tragic | Suspension of certain clauses within the document is permitted when in cases of rebellion or the public safety may require it | The canvas may be folded in on itself 7 times. A sheet of melinex is | laid over the area of loss on the landscape | not the face | dolled by what it would release.

Talking is a waste | product of thinking | budding from the wound surface | followed into folds. Click to open | your birthday | as a garden waking up | *There are no impervious skins or membranes in nature, no* | essay 'outlines'. Nothing is ever | the least part of anything. The safety word is | the safety word is | The past presents itself | elaborately dressed | in glass. Such trees are often colloquially referred to as 'husband and wife' trees, or 'marriage trees'. The tiles come away from | the transparent old wall behind the toys. The same area under different variables

alters

the number applied to the plot | the council building | internalises as a routine drill. Crying is a reassuring event and does not indicate distress. During the sermon, Bennett appeared very penitent, and was observed to weep and often shake his head, which were the outward signs of his inner sorrow and contrition. For although of | a weak enamel, the enforced | intimacy will surprise | Upon felicitations of failure | each voice, a rilling | of worn body facilities | fiddled above backward nodding branches | breakage re-enacted | at the waking part of June | necessary minerals | aroused.

There is nothing | left to miscarry | between chance | thoughts since | laughter leaning against | a covenant of | brickwork is distressed | by association. Hold your breath | up to the light it unfolds | in the shape of a swarm of birds | seen from below daydreams of | market indecision | as leisure. As if in thanksgiving it is possible | to hear when a bullet goes through its target | may have verbally led journalists [wrongly] out of the other side potentially going on to damage | the flowers, either human or hydraulic in the improvised field of | security. Let's call it

steve

its failure. To tamper | with the turning motion | is more informative than required. There must be a connexion between the great flavour of the crayfish and the manner in which the workers touch flaking skin. Despite protests issued by scholars | the transfusion became a dramatic, spiralling cone | from which it is difficult to distinguish a two-edged sword | and cut-and-paste or drag-and-drop operations | and to have interwoven them | in the web of Etiquettes | Embarrassments | And awes | a thought can lean against | to know what types of | distance it is not.

Traditionally, through the shopping centre | strode the child Ƿōden thc frontier was beyond. How did he keep himself in such happy shape? Like a tannoy in a rough climate, money | raining teeth pasting the dark | to the thread. Everything got so busy explaining other things to itself it really | Let yourself | into the field | for further instruction. It has been glued together | to make a compound patty deluxe | driven slumb'rous, snoring | through the corridors of your | Latin names | released. Despite the mirror, you are not

alone

I am here with you. In loneliness devotion | cries like a pliant limit clear a native term, almost anxious | to meet with what preceded uptaking of this single place | that was life, according to | ignoring the | And we've got that in common, the pigment | wished into being a location to return to as with flowers. Within it is its dependent margin | of little cubes in leisure | quiet as resemblance. The case is of signs to be developed in | strong teeth descending through the feed, mimed | light cross-legged in the trees | beneath cannot tell what time it is | downwards, and to the left.

For hours of boredom punctuated by moments of maxed-out sensory capacity | the dainty recruit sings to | avert the eyes from what we call extreme underload | in which looking is relief from not the face | interpretation | but steps from miles away | into the very last | Exhortations to a *Particular Repentance* | dressed suitably for enclosing animals. For all the riches he had acquired, van Dyck diminishes the ability of the sufferer to | cough, sputter and sneeze, mobilizing additional fluid | outside the limits | of the wilderness of repeated action | allowing the common man to have the

appearance

of elite status. The level experiencing | its name experienced the enjambment of | something pretending not to notice for fear of being walked away from, the way the sky treats everything like it should be happy to reflect it. Fuck that. Sufferance with | its yachty hide doubts the credentials of plainness, treating everything | that isn't treating blood | like blood like blood | is worse. The question mark steepens the snow's angle of approach | burying the triple tree. We live in plain sight of | low resolution hills | objects are travelling towards | to be touched | like mouths meeting | but by you.

Since every | bit is hallowed | contrition is waived | as time layered | around the eyes | weakening the parent filter precise objects pass through | unscathed. The level consists | devoid of weather | the present dancing | as sidebar. Like the one you have, only | forever? I would not be | deprived of the ability to quote unquote | break | dance. Knowing nothing but a vocabulary assembles | distress to deliver beneath these | a portrait of Major information becoming | falling objects out of which | a portrait is made, a helmet in Canterbury Cathedral it is possible to trace

a likeness

from | towards. I have driven | a trace between us | in the Flemish style, so that | It's always | stops | what is mean, you | Now to leave no, I | is always awake | as a flower springs | In a distant part of the colour. The days are soft | ly coming apart in the hand | as ice, divided | faintly describes a balustrade keeping | quote *locution* a part of its exclusion from what it might have | eventually, like mouths meeting | in the broken-down field | risen out of | again and again | to demonstrate | what it forgot to | become. In a distant part of the dream | of the square I forgot | to stop ending | for a change.

In the space of a few lines | intended for others | objects are travelling towards | by wave, you may mean | to establish | adjacent to a grief to pine | a copy failed by its origins. Like Christopher Newman, we signal intent | by curbs on 'pleasure' | analogous to nothing but sliproads | beaten out of a nail of the True Cross. Many of these are now known by administrative names | straight roads established by cont | inued use—a bollard, an ornamental planter, or concrete highway median. On that crystal-clear morning of mingled stuff | the breeze | feigned intimacy | where the

lines

used to be. Where the lines used to be | rooms sealing them from nothing. Derived from the sound of | crying, my mouth starts watering | auto-complete. There is loud music | behind the walls | within habit partially obscured by weather—protozoa in the water | moving my own hand | moving my own hand | across the water | To create the sign of | a toy. In a distant part of the square I came to observe | a better-than-exact replica of | Monmouth, the way the light | exceeds the absent border | articulation implies | patterns such as stained glass | to kneel openly, too convincingly | after.

No things were made | in the harming | of this settlement, opal scuttlebutts foreign to the dry pool | swum by red crops, a thing not to be touched but by you. The civic nothing is | desired by all, a statuette hemmed by | lakes, weekend knots within | pasture. Let the machines waltz | their immunity to the tune of | a garment Lee places around the | better-than-exact replica of | weather, a trace between evening | and soldiers. Thiersch | camps out, jingling with a star whip | newly troubled. We are so | sacred to be the first to discarded, Peckham raises | its tea dunes, lit

or

promoted by a sparrow. A square remains | clearing, as in 'softened' by the Scaffold | of discrete distances | marked by a fold | it is necessary to look upwards and | within to neglect. We were accumulating sleep as a prop | against technique, a thing not to be touched but | in hours, the communities dream | a residue left | like mouths meeting | on the surface of | the surface of | the street. Lacking surety, the names retreat | towards a taxonomy of names from which diminishing | walks its beat, a thing not to be | at most, an accompaniment to | the accompaniment of | whose feet.

OR AS

[7]

<table>
<tr><td>This is unsurprising.
The limitation of scope</td><td>It’s not surprising
The scope limitation</td></tr>
<tr><td>Comprehensive.</td><td>full</td></tr>
</table>

[14]

<table>
<tr><td>My goal is not to suggest
an imaginative construct
        discuss</td><td>My goal is not to suggest
an imaginative construct
        disgust</td></tr>
</table>

[16]

<table>
<tr><td>it’s important to note</td><td>It’s important to consider</td></tr>
<tr><td>to   sense</td><td>To feel</td></tr>
<tr><td>   balance
    as   tense</td><td>Balance
As stressed</td></tr>
<tr><td>   prematurity</td><td>badness</td></tr>
</table>

[20]

<table>
<tr><td> an unusual phenomenon</td><td>An exceptional occurrence</td></tr>
<tr><td>men</td><td>Me</td></tr>
<tr><td>   not remembering</td><td>Not remembering</td></tr>
<tr><td>the   discussion</td><td>What you said</td></tr>
</table>

[22]

lost in America and, sometimes paradox	Lost in America And sometimes Paradox
a desire fault	A wish Error

[23]

excellent friend	good friend
I want to propose	I want to make it
these convergences	These fusion
highlighted	prominent

[24]

their peculiar	They are special
richness	rich
irregular	irregular
producer of	Producer
flawed	defective
stems	towers

[28]

vividly Intensely
partial Loyal

porous Holy

handshake Greeting

a mixture of A combination of
monotony Similarities

[30]

the verbal images Language image
roots ground Root
just enough light Just enough light
to perceive contours Perceive contours

[31]

song for pleasure song for joy
Italian sculpture Italian sculpture
half-emergent being born
what is there what

[39]

blue seems Blue seems to be
legit legal

erosion erosion

in a mid 70s	in the mid-1970s
interior	indoor

[44]

combing my hair in a French room	Comb my hair In the French room
whisper	whisper it
autumn style fail	Fall style fail

[58]

failed to join	Failed to unpart
the sensitive sea	trembling sea
chatty	*Chatty*
with a capital P	And capital P

[64]

in the dream he turned away from the life of their time a line of trees	While he slept he rolled away from her body to check his phone

[67]

I don't know	I do not know
what they	What are they?

want me

to do

about

the darkness

over town

Want me

To do it

on

That darkness

In town

[68]

some imaginary
unhappinesses
in coalition

fictional
grievances
together at last

[70]

vulgar daydream

a hoisted basket

jukebox known by

antithesis

Vulgar daydreaming

A hanging basket

Automatic jukebox is known

Opposition

[78]

He was talking.
Two women. Three women.
The convention
was desperate

He was talking.
Two women, three women.
The convention
was desperate

[79]

<table>
<tr><td>Europe's debt</td><td>European debt</td></tr>
<tr><td>the dusk's rejoinder</td><td>Twilight's reverberation</td></tr>
<tr><td>a curious</td><td>Curious</td></tr>
<tr><td>lament</td><td>Lament</td></tr>
<tr><td>for bum notes</td><td>Burn notes</td></tr>
</table>

[81]

<table>
<tr><td>it's quite cool</td><td>That's cool</td></tr>
<tr><td>to trace</td><td>track</td></tr>
<tr><td>it's cool</td><td>This is cool</td></tr>
<tr><td>to trace</td><td>Tracking</td></tr>
<tr><td>it's quite cool to colour</td><td>Its cool colours</td></tr>
<tr><td>your eye</td><td>your eyes</td></tr>
</table>

[86]

<table>
<tr><td>poor folk</td><td>Poor</td></tr>
<tr><td>with old hats</td><td>With old hat</td></tr>
<tr><td></td><td></td></tr>
<tr><td>badly need</td><td>Very necessary</td></tr>
<tr><td></td><td></td></tr>
<tr><td>saturation</td><td>saturation</td></tr>
<tr><td></td><td></td></tr>
<tr><td>then to be plucked</td><td>And then pulled</td></tr>
<tr><td>smooth</td><td>smooth</td></tr>
</table>

[88]

<table>
<tr><td>I'll spend the summer</td><td>I will work</td></tr>
<tr><td>working on</td><td>in the summer</td></tr>
<tr><td></td><td></td></tr>
<tr><td>no</td><td>No</td></tr>
</table>

tasting

the sap of consciousness

Taste

Consciousness of the juice

[89]

an extraordinary toothpaste
bewildered ribbons
how you do it

Extraordinary toothpaste
Confused ribbon
How do you do

[91]

rhetorical selves
substitute selves
police selves
film selves
love and art selves

Rhetorical self
Replace oneself
The police themselves
The film itself
Love and art self

[93]

luminous bosses
lurking drums
marble veils
melted dreams
or half

Shiny boss
Diving drums
Marble veil
The dream of melting
Or half

[97]

the beauty of the genre
the cool mystery
the milk
the kindness

The attraction of the structure
The hot whodunnit
The milk
The kindness

[100]

The language of public life
intensely shabby
against the virtual

The external language
intensely tattered
by the virtual

[101]

we were captured in
the piano
naked and so luxurious

We were captured by
The piano
Nude and expensive

[102]

To die in the harbours
makes no
intelligible world
is elsewhere

To die in the harbours
makes nothing
intelligible of it
here

[103]

Hubris at the reverse piano
such particulars in the air

Hubris at the reverse piano
such details in the air

[104]

the dawn creeps
variables over
the snow in
hysteric stanzas

The dawn inches
changes over
the snow:
funny poem

[110]

the civil structures	Civilian structures
sewers	sewers
aqueducts	aqueducts
citadels	citadels
bridges	bridges
windows	the Windows

[111]

indeed but now be flattered a little for my pride puts all in doubt	effectively But now flattered a little For my pride puts all in doubt

[115]

The moment glimmers With what may cluster around it Green light Green autumn	The moment shines With what can be grouped around it Green light Green Fall

[119]

The last word is exhausted. Like a person We now hear so much of	The last word is out of print. As a person We hear so much

[124]

A footfall in the
speech. All is forgiven
outdated gibbering.

A passage in the
speech. Everything is forgiven.
Gibbering obsolete.

[129]

a toy theatre
blotted   blotted
and still I go on loving you

A theatre of toys
Crushed
And I still love you

[130]

The piano [unfolds or occurs].
You were not elected, yet

pear

The piano [unfolds or occurs].
You have not yet been elected

Perry

[140]

As   are
          and the
I   you
and   yet a   with
or   the   is
and even   as

In the same way
and the
I want you
And yet with
Where the
And even as

[143]

Life gets tedious …

arrow
          breast

Life becomes tedious …

arrow
breast

shirt

dollar
tuppence

check
check check check

shirt

dollar
tuppence

check
Check-in check

[144]

Love Poems
Cloudy Poems
Disinherited Poems
Dream Poems

Love poems
Cloud Poems
Poems Disinherited
Dream Poems

[145]

In the museum
standing among children
waiting
for clocks to chime

In the museum
Standing among
the waiting children
For carillon clocks

[146]

Paris to Zurich to Lausanne
to Paris to New York to
New York

Paris to Zurich to Lausanne
In Paris in New York for
New York

[148]

I can't remember
green a rich brown
turned to slate grey
with dusk or rain

I do not remember
Green a rich brown
Turned into slate grey
At dusk or rain

[153]

I love you
with my derogatory language.
Forgetting
as form?

I love you
With my derogatory language.
Oversight
As a form?

[155]

it had been raining
a delicate gesture
prove love
it had been rain

It was raining
A delicate gesture
Proving love
It had rained

[158]

pulling us
pulling us out
pulling us out of there
pulling us out

Attracting us
Removing
Getting out of there
Removing

[173]

The landscape echoed
blurrily; a general air
of carelessness.

The landscape echoed
vaguely; a general air
of errors.

[176]

Arnold pleads with the
cloud not to
cloud
cloud cloud
cloud cloud cloud
cloud

Arnold begs the
cloud not to
cloud
cloud cloud
cloud cloud
cloud cloud

cloud
cloud

cloud cloud

[177]

Ice waltzing
away from a structure
click bickering with the dark.

Ice waltzing
far from the structure
click the quarrels in the dark

[179]

There is some connexion—
we have it—no, wait
they have it—no, wait
no—

There is some connection.
We have it. No, wait.
They have it. No, wait.
No.

[182]

Oak leaves
Field Mice
Lakes
A sun
It all seems very English
to me

Oak leaves.
Field mice.
Lakes.
A sun.
It all seems very English
to me.

[183]

It will eventually lose the
attention of the others. The

It will eventually
lose the attention
of the others. The

[184]

waves and waves
of mint leaf

Waves and waves
of mint leaves.

easily discernible in attention.	Easily discernible inattention.

[187]

A small piece of diligence which bubbles up everywhere.	A small piece of diligence Which inflates all over.

[188]

Significant pre-echoes he taps into the flat and fenny land.	Important pre-echoes he taps into the flat and fenny ground.

[196]

Oh dear oh	Oh my God
I did in fact recognise the allusion Awkward	I have indeed recognised the allusion Embarrassing

[197]

doing these things	Doing these things
the other side of the coin	The other side of the room
jargon, on occasion	Jargon, occasionally

[199]

sailors

disciples

a bit of blatant biographical
glitter

Seamen

disciples

A blatant biographical
gun

[201]

the pun
like a prisoner
fascinated with the wall
of his cell

The pun
like a prisoner
fascinated by the wall
of his cell.

[202]

a long poem in which
some burning topic
is mentioned in every

a long poem in which
some burning
topic is mentioned in every

[203]

the delicious weightlessness
of George Osborne
swept gently aloft

the delicious lightness
of George Osborne
gently airlifted

[204]

I dally in the blizzard
the buoyancy of the blizzard

float float

I dawdle in the snowstorm
the snowstorm floats

floats floats

[206]

the soft focus
murmur of bees
murmurs of bees
in a megaphone

the imprecise
murmuring of bees
murmurings of bees
into a megaphone

[208]

this lofty view, for instance,
includes
Sunday and its seven
pressures

This sublime view, for example,

Sunday and its seven
pressures

[209]

hurrah

a plague of grace

hurrah

the season knits

hurrah

bloody chunks

hurray

A plague of grace

hurray

The season knits

hurray

Bloody pieces

[211]

wool roses
cool roses
symbolic roses
contemporary roses

Roses of wool
Fresh Roses
Symbolic Roses
Contemporary Roses

[212]

I hate it here, I hate it here,
I hate it here

I hate it here, I hate it here,
I hate it

please take

Takes Please

[214]

a nonce in a sonnet
a cork in a paddock
a gravity glass

A nuncio in a sonnet
A cork in a paddock
A gravity glass

[217]

strange meditative chants
moods and deals
stitched together
for small pay

Strange meditative songs
Moods & Offers
Sewn together
For a small salary

[219]

a gentle Georgian groan
in a disco version
sometime in May

A slight Georgian groan
In a disco version
In May

[220]

It occurs to me
it's now October
in the poem.

It seems to me
It is now October
In the poem.

To Naples!

In Naples!

[224]

a dumb rose
on a trampoline
a fresh if contradictory way

A mute rose
On a trampoline
A new way, so contradictory

[225]

our worst fears
are hoarded
in the spirit
their piecemeal shining

Our worst fears
Accumulated
In the spirit
Their fragmentary luster

[228]

alert to
an almost excessive fluency
with anxiety

Alert to
An almost excessive fluidity
With anxiety

[230]

I wish to keep my flowers
chirping
to keep sending them up
up there

I wish to keep my flowers
singing
To continue sending them
Yonder

[232]

the prickly feeling
the play
he seems actually to have lost
control of

The thorny feeling
the game
He appears to have lost
control of

[234]

the milkman
eating light
against the snow
a culture on a platter

The slag
Eat lightly
Against the snow
A culture on a plateau

[235]

the dolphins
the weasels
the horses
all kinds of shrieks
through the grating

the Dolphins
Butters
horses
All sorts of cries
Through the network

[241]

a practical joke
of canonicity
white rain
on the white wall

A practical joke
Canonicity
Light rain
On the white wall

[243]

my second hand absorbed it

shake it off
sh sh sh
shake it off

oh

My second hand absorbs it

shake
Sh sh sh
shake

Oh

BLOTTER

Unlike are we, unlike, O princely Heart!
Unlike our uses and our destinies.
—Elizabeth Barrett Browning

Without lifting the heel,
happiness, joy for the year,
Pulled, dragged along the ledges, circling faster
as a ghost cake.
Let physicians examine this phenomenon
such as bricks do not produce.
In the drowsy laziness
nothing, because you're so good
fell with disappointment.
And the mechanic, as luck would have
fun, unrestrained
but not out of love.
I would like to accommodate all the holiness of their
    teachings.
Summer is leaving us, Nikolai Blinov.

Curls shallow rivulet
and shine of the moon
I like to read aloud, and with an expression of mortality,
        notation, sermons
Tulips, spring steppe in bloom.
Coach Thomas Hogstedt,
do not belong.
At one and the same word is quite different meanings
In alternation
the word mystery already has a concept of hidden
and scattered a star.
What is the result? Look, here, for you. Down …
Let's go!
With torn thread beads.
And we are afraid: I think the price paid.

I was a friend of mine,
writes the poet in love.
And we cling to the animals, the soul is not empty
like a flashlight. No, wait!
Independence is scheduled for sanctions.
Psychic request
In the centre of the town square / all the doors are opened
stretched between 'doAmne' and 'vey'z world.'
Rain, ablution. Coin that pays for itself.
Bottomless puddle, six-foot closet,
she needs you. Lily of the valley in the shade, Lyudmila
        Kondratova,
I – a speck of dust,
the one who recognises your calling?
That's just the bees they are not a friendly race …

The mountains of garbage. THE SPRING!
Let all the way around. And by and by
We were together
Two ears, tongue and you present one
Loud cloud. But how long was your rock hidden in a kind
    of haze gray
Red sparrow
Ringing in the distance the snow.
Here such here pies with kittens
contrives to become ruler of the world, surrendering
    captured their ambitions
So you want to draw
Sky blue piece
To the far side?
Wags his tail, sprays sparks
in the snows of the volcano native

Feel the pulse of cloud
that there was, in the valley of the Three Rivers
Splash of wine with a little bit of wormwood
And the black will be snow.
All people are divided into healthy and those who consider
themselves sick.
Within days, serene cobwebs
full breath dreams
escalator of light fittings
Memory key
this color is blue, not blue!
Light in my house (Author: Natalia Stikine East)
Wake up again
rife with stars – with slide – it calotte.
And in the world again two moons

His life took place at a time when the power of the Tang
Empire, its shine
the seed has sprouted.
Mimicry – this is when you know all about, and you then
and there
look at the clouds
butterfly kiss
To the Milky Way, whenever escape
returning from the fair. It did not remember
Rhythms and mantras fly
break your heart
and outweighed by fence stakes
who know how to count money
Violet blooms. Anyone pick up a panacea.
It's somewhere on the pole, the world's steel
head ornaments

Absolutely not thinking why, just automatically,
she went to the old kennel.
At the door of each, my friend, there is a handle
and deadbolt
right, and he's right?'
For some reason this is necessary
But it is interesting ad nauseam.
Know! Kindness is such a thing
in puddles of dirty palette
learned from many years of fog.
Father Cherubino Kerub,
Hidden in the depths of a flower.
Gray ribbon of road …
I pulled out a gray hair.
With boats I beheld the mountains.
Emotions business does not take into account.

I cut off a piece of butcher on Shurpa
Did not lose heart and to 10h. Went to work in the morning.
In a past life he was an ass. Since the shell simply reversed
on the outskirts of
doors and … kind of tired of them is the same.
Yesterday we broke a date.
Ex-Premier of Belarus (Kebich).
All just nonsense, cherry brandy
Gestures and facial expressions
Then sings, cackles and chirps
Flute sound there
Emergency moon
And now sadness
Thousands of years already passed

Having children will understand me
standing on the table
fly in the clouds
granddaughters on my hands
I shuddered
Spacious thoughts. The weather gets warmer?
The boy was not twelve years old. And then he called his
Changed methods of struggle
weakly illuminating the darkness
your love waltz
in a piece of newspaper
wandering deer / form-fitting dress
Otherwise, do not feel the change.
Do not get lost in the branches.

Do not be an ass pocheshy
That's a very foamy beer now
through the open balcony
so it looks horrible
went. Puffy snow fell.
Looking for: support and oblivion.
Be strong in the aspen woodlands between the rocks.
On acne raskolina
You feel his cold hodgepodge
On crisp snow in the woods I go without fear.
See the imperfections in the darkness
Draw from the bucket
In the house of childhood and
For the flat edge of the earth according to Democritus

November

This is the first attempt at writing
from a suite of rooms
In a jealous company. Every day come new circulars
Following karma
bending winds
In the face of shocks. More!
Ukraine again began importing coal
I catch the bird of luck
In a flowing stream
They stand, and I imagine the food
turns pink cherry
Tell me, how do I find here the twin monsters?
Standing on tiptoe roses
attracted clouds and drove them away

The heart is deceitful. Only
a decline in gold reserves
Darkness in his eyes. Pain
A ray of sunshine ran
I will not Basho. I know that some things never say
crying over you so comfortable
and the smell of new fruit treasure
Broke into hundreds of fragments
They are always very varied
His uncontrollable mass.
The network has the video of the explosion CHP
suddenly met on the bridge
leave from the peak
Hot tea – lips burned itself – all forgotten

As a gift I'll take it
I kiss him and whisper.
Head-on collision: Mazda and Gazelle.
Here is another example of a false ceiling.
I would like to gnaw
even those I do not intend to continue to respect.
GDP bad times – all striving for a good chunk of the GDP.
He was not afraid, then he could think and decide.
Kettle my hand
In a cheerful mood like a business trip where we are
    desperately trying to get away from a quarrelsome
    wife.
At the top of the reshuffle
Soil moisture is saturated
How many thousands of years ago.
So cool rested on the job!

Recently clenched in ice
In the dream, see the ridiculous passion
Taking tenderness meetings and holy love of happiness
Look without falling down.
Here, in Paradise, for some unknown rules, true
This new nature does not create.
From your hands even poison, it will be as sweet.)) Such a positive and nice girl
like a dog sticking his head out the window
Death, reeking of incense
At the beginning of whinnying. Pig with a suitcase
took a 'test a bucket of ice water,' and you?
Happiness in the world
Qualitative review. Finally, and on a channel
I can't sleep.

What's the theme at the beginning of the Gamal? *September*
Inserting your logo in the video?
Yes, this 'disease' of all CO2 pistols from ASG:-(
Oil prices continued to rise on Friday afternoon
that would be productive training was needed to collect hair
in a ponytail really for 1.5 years
learned nothing
Everything was perfect
Immaculate Heart, streams of moisture
Boys were simply divine
It destroyed my brain
AGENT: Zayn Malik
OBJECTIVE: KILL Fundy
TIME: 6 seconds
MISSION COMPLETE

Panda, Art thou he
And you would be a word of ice installed on Pushkin Square?
Drawn by fast wave
one of them who really lies
Thank you, Helen. Beautiful image
HOW TO BREATHE
What do you think about Uncharted 4?
surprising that the opponent is itself not extinguished
A few questions: Who are they? Why are they without shoes? Why are they half naked? What they lost in a dumpster
He tried.
Cool shooting guys keep up the good work!!!!
oh what song song song what song aaa
I definitely every day
As you are our kids and not only? And what are the words at the bottom?

They normally do not pass
the main speaker does not rattle as a package
But sleeping areas are clean, fresh and green.
This is the new home of Jared. I can already imagine: –
Jared, why were you late? Yes, the house went out and got lost …
What do you call the first song?
The fish in the pond next to the house dinner.
Roofing, as it is
again I have nothing to do . . . I already feel dizzy
I love you. Very.
I almost burst out crying like a bitch ((((((((((
Did you know? Recently, scientists have found that strawberries contain substances that slow down the ageing
AAAAAAAA
That's not a smash
adjoining bedroom sleepy cry

Far away, in the mountains,
Tormented in the wilderness
and in the case of
breakfast squints
Let thine heart sing spring …
Seen in the pipe organ
and illuminated with light, realized
The cheaper the product, the more likely it is from China.
And what a song at the end???
He added: 'The Earth – not Heaven
Consumption of white paint and
Evening river
no longer worth it.
Figure you have, well, just a quiet horror.

September

There is something to be proud of. This schedule
of flights into space
Well, finally you can buy
Shiny on his chest Lily
Throw the link above lane 162
I just yell
I have a birthday today! I'm in Japan :(I hate this country.
What's the difference how old he is, who throws money? It
makes you not cold not hot.
I want this hair color. Or purple, or blue, or green.
German and Dutch journalists 'yelp'
In cassocks men with crosses
hahahahaha
All news Babe
Revising already 100,500 times
Waits for the Great Shaman to direct his gaze.

In the window, autumn
Actually happened to us.
Something happens . . .
I was rich – but became poor.
And Andryukha, mind all lines
overcome the gulf
already circled in the garden
and steep path untrodden.
But if you peer deeper
with the will to make friends
This squirrel
Rickets a joyful song.
Whose is it lonely sail
Nobody needs me :(

Not all elves left the local land *June*
and I hide them under different pretexts.
Gorky Park has become more beautiful, more attractive
        and convenient for a carefree holiday
'Who cares who, if not you?'
No one is currently lying
The air is filled With the scent of pine.
The whole world is in the small
That passed the fence.
Cash is enmity in literary circles.
After all, it confers the heavens.
'Not a soul made a blowjob...'
but, when you wait and heart
With her clothes
but so far everything's cool and I was very satisfied.

And so I live with him
suddenly and roam in the head
diffuse and not very relevant
Admiring the beauty of cherry blossoms.
Tries each
Here we go, and she says,
What do you want to tell me
Sonnet and its worthy ballad
So much to catch!
Thank you for your ancestors mind
But death perhaps not enough for all.
We stand with one foot in Europe and the other foot…
where?
I would sing a lullaby himself sprawled in the shade of
agaves.
Other people's prayers – always a burden.

I heard through the years
Weathervane on the dome, but blowing in the wrong
Night waiting on a dream.
Cry, friends
Still can not be dispersed
Or would have been sure of the response
Or I will send it or this is what I think.
And there is no farewell, and only this
Hedgehog on vacation at the beach.
'What does it matter who, if not you?'
So he thought, and was happy.
New task: Sell cabbage
Glass eyes
The shocking truth about the water and salt

September

Working life: when waking in the morning with difficulty
On the morning of January
frightened away a couple of pigeons
with the decision
Sometimes it is useful to be in the doghouse
But realizing that all life's adversities
Sleep on the heads of the flowers
after a thunderstorm and rain
Old people still die
So he thought
We close with the people
So hot lights
not a tank and infantry fighting vehicles
song lullaby

ACKNOWLEDGEMENTS

Thanks to the editors of the following publications, in which versions of some of these poems have previously appeared: *Clinic*, *Critical Quarterly*, *Currently & Emotion*, *Harper's*, *Maggy*, *Magma*, *PN Review*, *Poetry London*, *The Quietus*, *Test Centre*, *The White Review*. 'Within Habit' was published as a pamphlet by Test Centre in 2014, and 'Graig Syfyrddin, or Edmund's Tump' by If a Leaf Falls Press in 2017.